OVER VALES AND HILLS

The Illustrated Poetry of the Natural World

OVER VALES AND HILLS

The Illustrated Poetry of the Natural World

Selected by Fiona Waters

Photographs by the Daily Mail

Transatlantic Press

Published by Transatlantic Press in 2010.

Transatlantic Press
38 Copthorne Road
Croxley Green
Hertfordshire, WD3 4AQ, UK

All images © Associated Newspapers Archive
apart from pages 74 David Tipling/Photolibrary,
144 and 154 Mark Hamblin/Photolibrary
and 139 Getty Images.
This collection © Transatlantic Press 2010
Poems © the individual poets

ISBN 978-1-907176-18-0
Printed in China

CONTENTS

INTRODUCTION

I saw Eternity the other night
Like a great Ring of pure and endless light,
All calm as it was bright,
And round beneath it, Time in hours, days years
Driv'n by the spheres
Like a vast shadow mov'd, In which the world
And all her train were hurl'd;

Henry Vaughan 1621-1695

There was a time when Life was informed by nature, the earth's cycle drove the daily round of waking, working eating and sleeping. The great British preoccupation with the weather, the source of great derision to the rest of the world, may well have its roots in basic survival. The dark soul of the Bronte Sisters, the sharp and painful yet beautiful observation of AE Housman, the terrible beauty of WB Yeats, the inevitable tragedy of Thomas Hardy, a random selection of favourite poets which might say more about personal preferences, but must also reflect writers with the sensitivity to put in to words, for those less gifted, this close relationship we do all have with nature. And it is not only poets who have this insight; think of Gilbert White and Kilvert with their diaries and WH Hudson's A Shepherd's Life and John Moore's Brensham Trilogy.

There is a great bucolic tradition within poetry written in the English language. From Geoffrey Chaucer

Whan that Aprill with his shoures soote
The droghte of March hath perced to the roote
And bathed every veyne in swich licour,
Of which vertu engendred is the flowr
Whan Zephyrus eek with his sweete breeth
Inspired hath in every holt and heeth
The tendre croppes, and the yonge sonne
Hath in the Ram his halve cours yronne,
And smale foweles maken melodye
That slepen al the nyght with open ye
So priketh hem Nature in hir corages –
Thanne longen folk to goon on pilgrimages

through Andrew Marvell writing about glow-worms

Ye living Lamps, by whose dear light
The Nightingale does sit so late,
And studying all the Summer-night,
Her matchless Songs does meditate;

to William Wordsworth's very familiar

I wandered lonely as a cloud
That floats on high o'er vales and hills,
When all at once I saw a crowd,
A host, of golden daffodils;

The earliest poetry was focused on the beauteous benevolence of nature, the verdant countryside, the bountiful harvest, the teeming rivers, but equally on the dark other side of nature. The terrifying awe of eclipses, the sudden torrential and destructive rainfall, the huge fear of thunder and lightening. The intervention, as it was seen, of God as Pantocrator, far from kindly and hurling retribution down upon the wicked and sinful people.

The Romantics were a natural reaction to all this Sturm und Drang. All was idyllic and sylvan glades and flowers nodding in gentle zephyrs. The vision was so beguiling, so rich, it made poetry even more alive at a time when the wheels of the Industrial Revolution were churning and people were trapped in dark satanic mills so they yearned for the lost Eden which their forbears had known.

And so what of 21st century poets? Much of the poetry dealing with Nature from this century is chilling in its fleeting glimpses of paradise lost, the torrent of despair at the chaos mankind has wreaked upon this fragile earth. This fragile earth that when viewed from space is a glowing blue ball swathed in wreaths of white. Even urban supermarket man has to recognise the power of Nature when unleashed unexpectedly, be it a tsunami, a flood of biblical proportions, a crippling volcanic eruption or a drought so prolonged that vast lakes dry up, leaving behind earth deeply fissured and cracked, and crops ruined for generations to come. Our greatest technological advances can be rendered totally and utterly useless by one visitation from forces greater than ever imagined, because we have forgotten our small place in the grand scheme of things. For some people this is God driven, for others it is the eternal turning of the spheres. Beauty seen in the delicacy of a snowdrop appearing through the snow, beauty in the arcing rainbow after a summer shower, awesome beauty in a raging storm.

Fiona Waters
Dorset
August 2010

AND DID THOSE FEET IN ANCIENT TIME

And did those feet in ancient time
Walk upon England's mountains green?
And was the holy lamb of God
On England's pleasant pastures seen?

And did the countenance divine
Shine forth upon our clouded hills?
And was Jerusalem builded here
Among these dark Satanic mills?

Bring me my bow of burning gold!
Bring me my arrows of desire!
Bring me my spear – oh clouds unfold!
Bring me my chariot of fire!

I will not cease from mental fight
Nor shall my sword sleep in my hand,
Till we have built Jerusalem
In England's green and pleasant land.

William Blake

RIGHT: *Looking down over the White Horse at Bratton Camp, Wiltshire, 1934*

IN THE AIR

The buds return to twinkle the
stems and winter passes.
Time for the daffodils to raise
their yellow wine-glasses.

John Agard

LEFT: *Wild daffodils in Abbey Wood,*
Belvedere, Kent

RIGHT: *Cherry blossom in Sittingbourne,*
Kent, May 6, 1936

SPRING

Nothing is so beautiful as spring—
   When weeds, in wheels, shoot long and lovely and lush;
   Thrush's eggs look little low heavens, and thrush
Through the echoing timber does so rinse and wring
The ear, it strikes like lightnings to hear him sing;
   The glassy peartree leaves and blooms, they brush
   The descending blue; that blue is all in a rush
With richness ; the racing lambs too have fair their fling.

What is all this juice and all this joy?
   A strain of the earth's sweet being in the beginning
In Eden garden.—Have, get, before it cloy,
   Before it cloud, Christ, lord, and sour with sinning,
Innocent mind and Mayday in girl and boy,
   Most, O maid's child, thy choice and worthy the winning.

Gerard Manley Hopkins

LEFT: *Langdale Pikes, April 15, 1938*

RIGHT: *Cherry blossom in Great Kingshill, Buckinghamshire, April 29, 1935.*

FAREWELL

Farewell to the bushy clump close to the river
And the flags where the butter-bump hides in forever;
Farewell to the weedy nook, hemmed in by waters;
Farewell to the miller's brook and his three bonny daughters;
Farewell to them all while in prison I lie –
In the prison a thrall sees naught but the sky.

Shut out are the green fields and birds in the bushes;
In the prison yard nothing builds, blackbirds or thrushes.
Farewell to the old mill and dash of waters,
To the miller and, dearer still, to his three bonny daughters.

In the nook, the larger burdock grows near the green willow;
In the flood, round the moor-cock dashes under the billow;
To the old mill farewell, to the lock, pens, and waters,
To the miller himsel', and his three bonny daughters.

John Clare

LEFT: *Llanwrytd Brecon*

ABOVE: *The Chess Valley, Latimer, Buckinghamshire, April 30, 1936*

DOVER BEACH

The sea is calm tonight
The tide is full, the moon lies fair
Upon the straits; on the French coast the light
Gleams and is gone; the cliffs of England stand,
Glimmering and vast, out in the tranquil bay.
Come to the window, sweet is the night air!
Only, from the long line of spray
Where the sea meets the moon-blanched land,
Listen! you hear the grating roar
Of pebbles which the waves draw back, and fling,
At their return, up the high strand,
Begin, and cease, and then again begin,
With tremulous cadence slow, and bring
The eternal note of sadness in.
Sophocles long ago
Heard it on the Aegean, and it brought
Into his mind the turbid ebb and flow
Of human misery; we
Find also in the sound a thought,

Hearing it by this distant northern sea.
The Sea of Faith
Was once, too, at the full, and round earth's shore
Lay like the folds of a bright girdle furled.
But now I only hear
Its melancholy, long, withdrawing roar,
Retreating, to the breath
Of the night wind, down the vast edges drear
And naked shingles of the world.
Ah, love, let us be true
To one another! for the world, which seems
To lie before us like a land of dreams,
So various, so beautiful, so new,
Hath really neither joy, nor love, nor light,
Nor certitude, nor peace, nor help for pain;
And we are here as on a darkling plain
Swept with confused alarms of struggle and flight,
Where ignorant armies clash by night.

Matthew Arnold

THE BURNING OF THE LEAVES

Now is the time for the burning of the leaves,
They go to the fire; the nostrils prick with smoke
Wandering slowly into the weeping mist.
Brittle and blotched, ragged and rotten sheaves!
A flame seizes the smouldering ruin, and bites
On stubborn stalks that crackle as they resist.
The last hollyhock's fallen tower is dust:
All the spices of June are a bitter reek,
All the extravagant riches spent and mean.
All burns! the reddest rose is a ghost.
Spark whirl up, to expire in the mist: the wild
Fingers of fire are making corruption clean.
Now is the time for stripping the spirit bare,
Time for the burning of days ended and done,
Idle solace of things that have gone before,
Rootless hope and fruitless desire are there:
Let them go to the fire with never a look behind.
That world that was ours is a world that is ours no more.
They will come again, the leaf and the flower, to arise
From squalor of rottenness into the old splendour,
And magical scents to a wondering memory bring;
The same glory, to shine upon different eyes.
Earth cares for her own ruins, naught for ours.
Nothing is certain, only the certain spring.

Laurence Binyon

RIGHT: *High Beech, Epping Forest, September 1, 1933*

UPPER LAMBOURNE

Up the ash tree climbs the ivy,
Up the ivy climbs the sun,
With a twenty-thousand pattering,
Has a valley breeze begun,
Feathery ash, neglected elder,
Shift the shade and make it run –

Shift the shade toward the nettles,
And the nettles set it free
To streak the stained Carrara headstone
Where, in nineteen-twenty-three,
He who trained a hundred winners
Paid the Final Entrance Fee.

Leathery limbs of Upper Lambourne,
Leathery skin from sun and wind,
Leathery breeches, spreading stables,
Shining saddles left behind –
To the down the string of horses
Moving out of sight and mind.

Feathery ash in leathery Lambourne
Waves above the sarsen stone,
And Edwardian plantations
So coniferously moan
As to make the swelling downland,
Far surrounding, seem their own.

John Betjeman

ABOVE: *Newbury, Berkshire, June 23, 1997*   RIGHT: *Ivinghoe Beacon, Buckinghamshire, April 3, 1936*

LONDON SNOW

When men were all asleep the snow came flying,
In large white flakes falling on the city brown,
Stealthily and perpetually settling and loosely lying,
 Hushing the latest traffic of the drowsy town;
Deadening, muffling, stifling its murmurs failing;
Lazily and incessantly floating down and down:
 Silently sifting and veiling road, roof and railing;
Hiding difference, making unevenness even,
Into angles and crevices softly drifting and sailing.
 All night it fell, and when full inches seven
It lay in the depth of its uncompacted lightness,
The clouds blew off from a high and frosty heaven;
 And all woke earlier for the unaccustomed brightness
Of the winter dawning, the strange unheavenly glare:
The eye marvelled – marvelled at the dazzling whiteness;
 The ear hearkened to the stillness of the solemn air;
No sound of wheel rumbling nor of foot falling,
And the busy morning cries came thin and spare.
 Then boys I heard, as they went to school, calling,
They gathered up the crystal manna to freeze
Their tongues with tasting, their hands with snowballing;
 Or rioted in a drift, plunging up to the knees;
Or peering up from under the white-mossed wonder,

'O look at the trees!' they cried, 'O look at the trees!'
With lessened load a few carts creak and blunder,
Following along the white deserted way,
A country company long dispersed asunder:
 When now already the sun, in pale display
Standing by Paul's high dome, spread forth below
His sparkling beams, and awoke the stir of the day.
 For now doors open, and war is waged with the snow;
And trains of sombre men, past tale of number,
Tread long brown paths, as toward their toil they go:
 But even for them awhile no cares encumber
Their minds diverted; the daily word is unspoken,
The daily thoughts of labour and sorrow slumber
At the sight of the beauty that greets them, for the charm
they have broken.

Robert Bridges

HOME THOUGHTS
FROM ABROAD

Oh, to be in England
Now that April's there,
And whoever wakes in England
Sees, some morning, unaware,
That the lowest boughs and the brushwood sheaf
Round the elm-tree bole are in tiny leaf,
While the chaffinch sings on the orchard bough
In England—now!
And after April, when May follows,
And the whitethroat builds, and all the swallows!
Hark, where my blossom'd pear-tree in the hedge
Leans to the field and scatters on the clover
Blossoms and dewdrops—at the bent spray's edge—
That's the wise thrush; he sings each song twice over
Lest you should think he never could recapture
The first fine careless rapture!
And though the fields look rough with hoary dew,
All will be gay when noontide wakes anew
The buttercups, the little children's dower,
—Far brighter than this gaudy melon-flower!

Robert Browning

RIGHT: *The Cleeve valley, River Tamar, Cornwall*

TO A MOUSE

Wee, sleeket, cowran, tim'rous beastie,
O, what a panic's in thy breastie!
Thou need na start awa sae hasty
Wi bickering brattle!
I wad be laith to rin an' chase thee,
Wi' murd'ring pattle.

I'm truly sorry man's dominion
Has broken nature's social union,
An' justifies that ill opinion
Which makes thee startle
At me, thy poor, earth-born companion
An' fellow mortal!

I doubt na, whyles, but thou may thieve;
What then? poor beastie, thou maun live!
A daimen-icker in a thrave
'S a sma' request;
I'll get a blessin wi' the lave,
An' never miss't.

Thy wee-bit housie, too, in ruin!
It's silly wa's the win's are strewin!
An' naething, now, to big a new ane,
O' foggage green!
An' bleak December's wind's ensuin,
Baith snell an' keen!

Thou saw the fields laid bare an' waste,
An' weary winter comin fast,
An' cozie here, beneath the blast,
Thou thought to dwell,
Till crash! the cruel coulter passed
Out thro' thy cell.

That wee-bit heap o' leaves an' stibble,
Has cost thee monie a weary nibble!
Now thou's turned out, for a' thy trouble,
But house or hald,
To thole the winter's sleety dribble,
An' cranreuch cauld.

But mousie, thou art no thy-lane,
In proving foresight may be vain:
The best-laid schemes o' mice an' men
Gang aft agley,
An' lea'e us nought but grief an' pain,
For promis'd joy!

Still thou are blessed, compared wi' me!
The present only toucheth thee:
But och! I backward cast my e'e,
On prospects drear!
An' forward, tho' I canna see,
I guess an' fear!

Robert Burns

THE OVEN BIRD

There is a singer everyone has heard,
Loud, a mid-summer and a mid-wood bird,
Who makes the solid tree trunks sound again.
He says that leaves are old and that for flowers
Mid-summer is to spring as one to ten.
He says the early petal-fall is past,
When pear and cherry bloom went down in showers
On sunny days a moment overcast;
And comes that other fall we name the fall.
He says the highway dust is over all.
The bird would cease and be as other birds
But that he knows in singing not to sing.
The question that he frames in all but words
Is what to make of a diminished thing.

Robert Frost

LEFT: *A view of Savernake Forest, January 27, 1929*

THE PROLOGUE TO THE CANTERBURY TALES

(extract)

Whan that Aprille, with hise shoures sote,
The droghte of Marche hath perced to the rote
And bathed every veyne in swich licour,
Of which vertu engendred is the flour;
Whan Zephirus eek with his swete breeth
Inspired hath in every holt and heeth
The tendre croppes, and the yonge sonne
Hath in the Ram his halfe cours y-ronne,
And smale fowles maken melodye,
That slepen al the night with open eye–
So priketh hem nature in hir corages–
Than longen folk to goon on pilgrimages
And palmers for to seken straunge strondes
To ferne halwes, kowthe in sondry londes
And specially, from every shires ende
Of Engelond, to Caunterbury they wende,
The holy blisful martir for to seke,
That hem hath holpen, whan that they were seke.

Geoffrey Chaucer

BELOW: King Arthur's Seat, Berkshire   RIGHT: *Church at Shillington, Bedfordshire*

34

WINTER IN THE FENS

So moping flat and low our valleys lie
So dull and muggy is our winter sky
Drizzling from day to day dull threats of rain
And when that falls still threating on again
From one wet week so great an ocean flows
That every village to an island grows
And every road for even weeks to come
Is stopt and none but horsemen go from home
And one wet night leaves travels best in doubt
And horseback travel asks if floods are out
Such are the lowland scenes that winter gives
And strangers wonder where our pleasure lives
Yet in a little garden close at home
I watch for spring and there the crocus comes
And in a little close however keen

The winter comes I find a patch of green
And then mayhap a letter from a friend
Just in the bustle of the city penned
And then to show that friendships warmth survives
The winter from the busy town arrives
A letter spite the flooded roads – with news
– New books old friendships authors and reviews
While the intermediate blanks employ
And though fenced in with water meet with joy
Though troubled waters down the meadow roars
And fancy dreads the danger out of doors
When every little window after dark
Lights comfort in like faith in noahs ark

John Clare

BELOW: *Winter in Perthshire, February 3, 1937*

WOLF

A wolf is reading a book of fairy tales.
The moon hangs over the forest, a lamp.
He is not assuming a human position,
say, cross-legged against a tree,
as he would in a cartoon.
This is a real wolf, standing on all fours,
his rich fur bristling in the night air,
his head bent over the book open on the ground.
He does not sit down for the words
would be too far away to be legible,
and it is with difficulty that he turns
each page with his nose and forepaws.
When he finishes the last tale
he lies down in pine needles.
He thinks about what he has read,
the stories passing over his mind,
like the clouds crossing the moon.
A zigzag of wind shakes down hazelnuts.
The eyes of owls yellow in the branches.
The wolf now paces restlessly in circles
around the book until he is absorbed
by the power of its narration,
making him one of its illustrations,
a small paper wolf, flat as print.
Later that night, lost in a town of pigs,
he knocks over houses with his breath.

Billy Collins

RIGHT: *Aviemore, Cairngorm Mountains*

THE SONG OF WANDERING AENGUS

I went out to the hazel wood,
Because a fire was in my head,
And cut and peeled a hazel wand,
And hooked a berry to a thread;
And when white moths were on the wing,
And moth-like stars were flickering out,
I dropped the berry in a stream
And caught a little silver trout.

When I had laid it on the floor
I went to blow the fire aflame,
But something rustled on the floor,
And some one called me by my name.
It had become a glimmering girl
With apple blossom in her hair
Who called me by my name and ran
And faded through the brightening air.

Though I am old with wandering
Through hollow lands and hilly lands.
I will find out where she has gone,
And kiss her lips and take her hands;
And walk among long dappled grass,
And pluck till time and times are done
The silver apples of the moon,
The golden apples of the sun.

William Butler Yeats

ABOVE: *Stile on the summit of Churchdown, Gloucestershire.*

LEFT: *The Wye Valley*

A DIFFICULT BIRTH, EASTER 1998

An old ewe that somehow till this year
had given the ram the slip. We thought her barren.
Good Friday, and the Irish peace deal close,
and tonight she's serious, restless and hoofing the straw.
We put off the quiet supper and bottle of wine
we'd planned, to celebrate if the news is good.

Her waters broke an hour ago and she's sipped
her own lost salty ocean from the ground.
While they slog it out in Belfast, eight decades
since Easter 1916, exhausted, tamed by pain,
she licks my fingers with a burning tongue.
lies down again. Two hooves and a muzzle.

But the lamb won't come. You phone for help
and step into the lane to watch for car lights.
This is when the whitecoats come to the women,
well-meaning, knowing best, with their needles and forceps.
So I ease my fingers in, take the slippery head
in my right hand, two hooves in my left.

We strain together, harder than we dared.
I feel a creak in the limbs and pull till he comes
in a syrupy flood. She drinks him, famished, and you find us
peaceful, at a cradling that might have been a death.
Then the second lamb slips through her opened door,
the stone rolled away.

Gillian Clarke

RIGHT: *Ben Nevis, April 11, 1935*

IN THE EVENING

The heads of roses begin to droop.
The bee who has been hauling his gold
All day finds a hexagon in which to rest.

In the sky, traces of clouds,
The last few darting birds,
watercolors on the horizon

The white cat sits facing a wall.
The horse in the field is asleep on its feet.

I light a candle on the wood table.
I take another sip of wine.
I pick up an onion and a knife.

And the past and the future?
Nothing but an only child with two different masks.

Billy Collins

BELOW: *Sunset, April 13, 1936*   RIGHT: *Moon rising over the Caledon River in Basutoland, South Africa, April 3, 1934*

THE MAN IN THE MOON

He used to frighten me in the nights
of childhood,
the wide adult face, enormous, stern, aloft
I could not imagine such loneliness, such coldness
But tonight as I drive home over
these hilly roads
I see him sinking behind stands of winter trees
And rising again to show his familiar face
And when he comes into full view
over open fields
he looks like a young man who has fallen in love
with the dark earth
a pale bachelor, well-groomed and
full of melancholy
his round mouth open
as if he had just broken into song.

Billy Collins

FLOWERS

Some men never think of it.
You did. You'd come along
And say you'd nearly brought me flowers
But something had gone wrong.

The shop was closed. Or you had doubts –
The sort that minds like ours
Dream up incessantly. You thought
I might not want your flowers.

It made me smile and hug you then.
Now I can only smile.
But, look, the flowers you nearly brought
Have lasted all this while.

Wendy Cope

BELOW: *Tulips in Spalding, May 12, 1957.*

LINES WRITTEN IN EARLY SPRING

I heard a thousand blended notes
While in a grove I sat reclined
In that sweet mood when pleasant thoughts
Bring sad thoughts to the mind.

To her fair works did nature link
The human soul that through me ran,
And much it grieved my heart to think
What man has made of man.

Through primrose tufts, in that green bower,
The periwinkle trailed its wreaths;
And 'tis my faith that every flower
Enjoys the air it breathes.

The birds around me hopped and played,
Their thoughts I cannot measure,
But the least motion which they made
It seemed a thrill of pleasure.

The budding twigs spread out their fan,
To catch the breezy air;
And I must think, do all I can,
That there was pleasure there.

If this belief from heaven be sent,
If such be Nature's holy plan,
Have I not reason to lament
What man has made of man?

William Wordsworth

48   RIGHT: *Apple blossom in Farningham, Kent, May 10, 1939*

HIGH SUMMER ON THE MOUNTAINS

High summer on the mountains
And on the clover leas,
And on the local sidings,
And on the rhubarb leaves.

Brass bands in all the valleys
Blaring defiant tunes,
Crowds, acclaiming carnival,
Prize pigs and wooded spoons

Dust on shabby hedgerows
Behind the colliery wall,
Dust on rail and girder
And tram and prop and all.

High summer on the slag heaps
And on polluted streams,
And old men in the morning
Telling the town their dreams.

Idris Davies

LEFT: *Dovedale*

GREEN MAN IN THE GARDEN

Green man in the garden
Staring from the tree,
Why do you look so long and hard
Through the pane at me?
Your eyes are dark as holly
Of sycamore your horns,
Your bones are made of elder branch,
Your teeth are made of thorns.

Your hat is made of ivy-leaf
Of bark your dancing shoes,
And evergreen and green and green
Your jacket and shirt and trews.

Leave your house and leave your land and throw away the key,
And never look behind, he creaked
And come and live with me.

I bolted up the window, I bolted up the door,
I drew the blind that I should find the green man never more.

But when I softly turned the stair
As I went up to bed,
I saw the green man standing there.
'Sleep well, my friend,' he said.

Charles Causley

ABOVE: *Shillington, Bedfordshire*

SILVER

Slowly, silently, now the moon
Walks the night in her silver shoon;
This way, and that, she peers, and sees
Silver fruit upon silver trees;
One by one the casements catch
Her beams beneath the silvery thatch;
Couched in his kennel, like a log,
With paws of silver sleeps the dog;
From their shadowy cote the white breasts peep
Of doves in silver-feathered sleep
A harvest mouse goes scampering by,
With silver claws, and silver eye;
And moveless fish in the water gleam,
By silver reeds in a silver stream.

Walter de la Mare

LEFT: *River Poulton in Clumber Park, Nottinghamshire.*

NURSE'S SONG
(SONGS OF INNOCENCE)

When the voices of children are heard on the green
And laughing is heard on the hill,
My heart is at rest within my breast
And everything else is still.

'Then come home, my children, the sun is gone down,
And the dews of night arise;
Come come leave off play, and let us away
Till the morning appears in the skies.'

'No no let us play, for it is yet day,
And we cannot go to sleep;
Besides in the sky the little birds fly
And the hills are all covered with sheep.'

'Well well, go and play till the light fades away
And then go home to bed.'
The little ones leaped and shoutèd, and laughed
And all the hills echoed.

William Blake

RIGHT: *Kew Gardens, February 16, 1948*

ABOVE: *Stonehenge, Wiltshire*

TO EARTHWARD

Love at the lips was touch
As sweet as I could bear;
And once that seemed too much;
I lived on air

That crossed me from sweet things,
The flow of – was it musk
From hidden grapevine springs
Downhill at dusk?

I had the swirl and ache
From sprays of honeysuckle
That when they're gathered shake
Dew on the knuckle.

I craved strong sweets, but those
Seemed strong when I was young;
The petal of the rose
It was that stung.

Now no joy but lacks salt,
That is not dashed with pain
And weariness and fault;
I crave the stain

Of tears, the aftermark
Of almost too much love,
The sweet of bitter bark
And burning clove.

When stiff and sore and scarred
I take away my hand
From leaning on it hard
In grass and sand,

The hurt is not enough:
I long for weight and strength
To feel the earth as rough
To all my length.

Robert Frost

THE FALLOW DEER AT
THE LONELY HOUSE

One without looks in tonight
  Through the curtain-chink
From the sheet of glistening white;
One without looks in tonight
  As we sit and think
  By the fender-brink.

We do not discern those eyes
  Watching in the snow;
Lit by lamps of rosy dyes
We do not discern those eyes
  Wondering, aglow
  Four-footed, tiptoe.

Thomas Hardy

ABOVE: *Deer in Richmond Park*   RIGHT: *Entrance to Dovedale and Bunster Hill, Staffordshire*

THE POPLAR FIELD

The poplars are felled, farewell to the shade
And the whispering sound of the cool colonnade
The winds play no longer and sing in the leaves,
Nor Ouse on his bosom their image receives.

Twelve years have elapsed since I first took a view
Of my favourite field, and the bank where they grew,
And now in the grass behold they are laid,
And the tree is my seat that once lent me a shade.

The blackbird has fled to another retreat
Where the hazels afford him a screen from the heat
And the scene where his melody charmed me before
Resounds with his sweet-flowing ditty no more.

My fugitive years are all hasting away,
And I must e're long lie as lowly as they,
With a turf on my breast and a stone at my head
E're another such grove shall arise in its stead.

'Tis a sight to engage me, if anything can,
To muse on the perishing pleasures of Man;
Short-lived as we are, our enjoyments, I see,
Have a still shorter date, and die sooner than we.

Willam Cowper

And then to awake, and the farm, like a wanderer white
With the dew, come back, the cock on his shoulder: it was all
Shining, it was Adam and maiden,
The sky gathered again
And the sun grew round that very day,
So it must have been after the birth of the simple light
In the first, spinning place, the spellbound horses walking warm
Out of the whinnying green stable
On to the fields of praise.

And honoured among foxes and pheasants by the gay house
Under the new made clouds and happy as the heart was long,
In the sun born over and over,
I ran my heedless ways,
My wishes raced through the house high hay
And nothing I cared, at my sky blue trades, that time allows
In all his tuneful turning so few and such morning songs
Before the children green and golden
Follow him out of grace.

Nothing I cared, in the lamb white days, that time would take me
Up to the swallow thronged loft by the shadow of my hand,
In the moon that is always rising,
Nor that riding to sleep
I should hear him fly with the high fields
And wake to the farm forever fled from the childless land.
Oh as I was young and easy in the mercy of his means,
Time held me green and dying
Though I sang in my chains like the sea.

Dylan Thomas

IN MEMORIAM

(Extract)

Calm is the morn without a sound,
Calm as to suit a calmer grief,
And only thro' the faded leaf
The chestnut pattering to the ground:

Calm and deep peace on this high wold,
And on these dews that drench the furze,
And all the silvery gossamers
That twinkle into green and gold:

Calm and still light on yon great plain
That sweeps with all its autumn bowers,
And crowded farms and lessening towers,
To mingle with the bounding main:

Calm and deep peace in this wide air,
These leaves that redden to the fall;
And in my heart, if calm at all,
If any calm, a calm despair:

Calm on the seas, and silver sleep,
And waves that sway themselves in rest,
And dead calm in that noble breast
Which heaves but with the heaving deep.

Alfred, Lord Tennyson

RIGHT: *Dinmore Hill, Herefordshire, September 25, 1936*

STOPPING BY WOODS ON A SNOWY EVENING

Whose woods these are I think I know.
His house is in the village, though;
He will not see me stopping here
To watch his woods fill up with snow.

My little horse must think it queer
To stop without a farmhouse near
Between the woods and frozen lake
The darkest evening of the year.

He gives his harness bells a shake
To ask if there is some mistake.
The only other sound's the sweep
Of easy wind and downy flake.

The woods are lovely, dark, and deep,
But I have promises to keep,
And miles to go before I sleep,
And miles to go before I sleep.

Robert Frost

THE STARLIGHT NIGHT

Look at the stars! look, look up at the skies!
 O look at all the fire-folk sitting in the air!
 The bright boroughs, the circle-citadels there!
Down in dim woods the diamond delves! the elves'-eyes!
The grey lawns cold where gold,
where quickgold lies!
 Wind-beat whitebeam! airy abeles set on a flare!
 Flake-doves sent floating forth at a farmyard scare!
Ah well! it is all a purchase, all is a prize.

Buy then! bid then! – What? – Prayer, patience, alms, vows.
Look, look: a May-mess, like on orchard boughs!
 Look! March-bloom, like on mealed-with-yellow sallows!
These are indeed the barn; withindoors house
The shocks. This piece-bright paling shuts the spouse
 Christ home, Christ and his mother and all his hallows.

Gerard Manley Hopkins

LEFT: *Early morning on Wimbledon Common, February 21, 1934*

RIGHT: *Tolcarne Beach, Newquay, July 13, 1937*

HARVEST

They were summers full of sunshine. In the fields
we would creep into the stooks of tilted sheaves,
crouching with scratched legs
among the sharp-cut stubble. Tight to dry earth
too low for blades to catch grew speedwell
blue as cornflower, pimpernel
red as poppy.

From two-tined shining forks, long handles worn
to patina by hard balms, the sheaves flew high
onto carts lead-red and blue-sky painted.
The wheels rolled heavy-hubbed and iron-rimmed
weightily field to stack and lighter back again
between straw-littered hedges dull with dust.

As the day drooped to evening we'd ride the wide backs
of Boxer or Diamond to the farmyard. Freed from shafts,
greasy black straps swinging, they could wade
into the pond, drink, bend their great necks.
it was the men's joke not to lift us down
but thwack the chestnut rumps, send us to balance
above the surface smeared with sap-green weed.
They teased us, town children, made us brave;
and I remember them, the faces, names, speech,
working clothes and movements of those men,
the perks they carried home; skimmed milk in cans,
field cabbages in sacks, soft rabbits
swinging head-down from loops of twine, to feed
long families of uncombed dusty children
who stood at laneside gates,
watched us without a smile.

Pamela Gillilan

LEFT: *Harvesting in Essex, August 6, 1936*

RIGHT: *Farmers thresh and bale their hay, Barkway, Hertfordshire, August 19, 1936*

THE KINGFISHER

The Kingfisher perches. He studies.

Escaped from the jeweller's opium
X-rays the river's toppling
Tangle of glooms.

Now he's vanished – into vibrations.
A sudden electric wire, jarred rigid,
Snaps – with a blue flare.

He has left his needle buried in your ear.

Oakfish oaks, kneeling, bend over
Dragging with their reflections
For the sunken stones. The Kingfisher
Erupts through the mirror, beak full of ingots,

A spilling armful of gems, beak full of ingots,
And is away – cutting the one straight line
Of the raggle-taggle tumbledown river
With a diamond –

Leaves a rainbow splinter sticking in your eye.

Through him, God, whizzing in the sun,
Glimpses the angler.

Through him, God
Marries a pit
Of fishy mire.
            And look! He's
– gone again.
                        Spark, sapphire, refracted
From beyond water
Shivering the spine of the river.

Ted Hughes

BADGERS

When the badger glimmered away
into another garden
you stood, half-lit with whiskey,
sensing you had disturbed
some soft returning.

The murdered dead,
you thought.
But could it not have been
some violent shattered boy
nosing out what got mislaid
between the cradle and the explosion,
evenings when windows stood open
and the compost smoked down the backs?

Visitations are taken for signs.
At a second house I listened
for duntings under the laurels
and heard intimations whispered
about being vaguely honoured.

And to read even by carcasses
the badgers have come back.
One that grew notorious
lay untouched in the roadside.
Last night one had me braking
but more in fear than in honour.

Cool from the sett and redolent
of his runs under the night,
the bogey of fern country
broke cover in me
for what he is:
pig family
and not at all what he's painted.

How perilous is it to choose
not to love the life we're shown?
His sturdy dirty body
and interloping grovel.
the intelligence in his bone.
the unquestionable houseboy's shoulders
that could have been my own.

Seamus Heaney

LEFT: *Savernake Forest, Wiltshire.*

TO THE VIRGINS, TO MAKE MUCH OF TIME

Gather ye rosebuds while ye may,
Old Time is still a-flying:
And this same flower that smiles today
Tomorrow will be dying.

The glorious Lamp of Heaven, the Sun,
The higher he's a-getting,
The sooner will his race be run,
And neerer he's to setting.

That age is best, which is the first,
When youth and blood are warmer;
But being spent, the worse, and worst
Times, still succeed the former.

Then be not coy, but use your time,
And while ye may, go marry:
For having lost but once your prime,
You may for ever tarry.

Robert Herrick

BELOW: *Sunset, July, 1931*　　RIGHT: *Amid the bracken, Epping Forest, November 20, 1938*

MIST IN THE MEADOWS

The evening oer the meadow seems to stoop

More distant lessens the diminished spire

Mist in the hollows reaks and curdles up

Like fallen clouds that spread – and things retire

Less seen and less – the shepherd passes near

And little distant most grotesquely shades

As walking without legs – lost to his knees

As through the rawky creeping smoke he wades

Now half way up the arches disappear

And small the bits of sky that glimmer through

Then trees loose all but tops – I meet the fields

And now the indistinctness passes bye

The shepherd all his length is seen again

And further on the village meets the eye

John Clare

RIGHT: *Salisbury Plain, 1936*

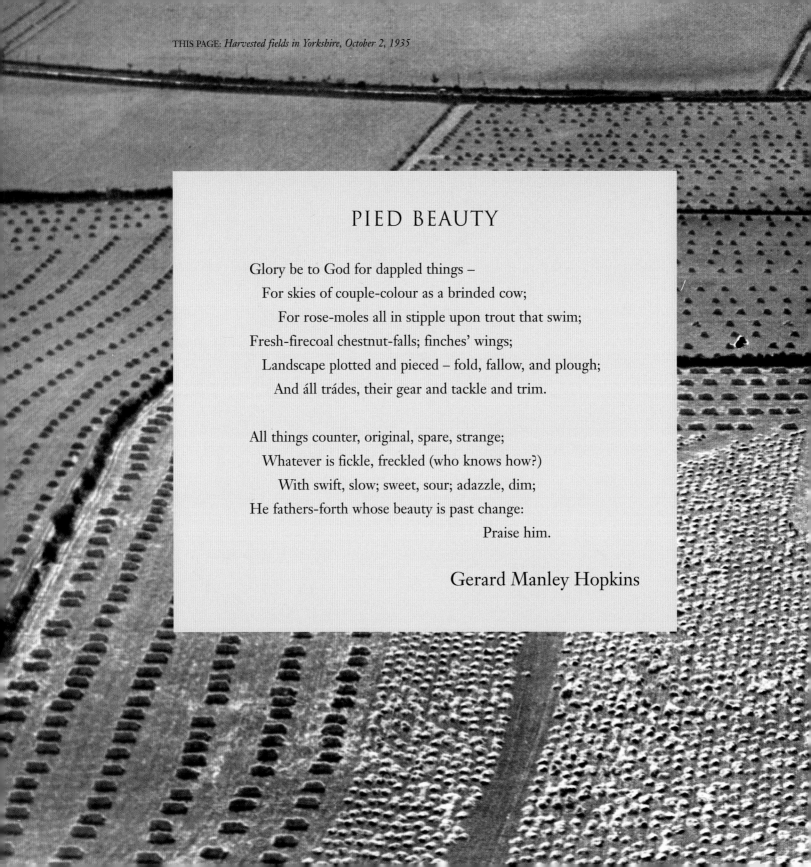

PIED BEAUTY

Glory be to God for dappled things –
   For skies of couple-colour as a brinded cow;
     For rose-moles all in stipple upon trout that swim;
Fresh-firecoal chestnut-falls; finches' wings;
   Landscape plotted and pieced – fold, fallow, and plough;
     And áll trádes, their gear and tackle and trim.

All things counter, original, spare, strange;
   Whatever is fickle, freckled (who knows how?)
     With swift, slow; sweet, sour; adazzle, dim;
He fathers-forth whose beauty is past change:
             Praise him.

Gerard Manley Hopkins

LOVELIEST OF TREES, THE CHERRY NOW

Loveliest of trees, the cherry now
Is hung with bloom along the bough,
And stands about the woodland ride
Wearing white for Eastertide.

Now, of my threescore years and ten,
Twenty will not come again,
And take from seventy springs a score,
It only leaves me fifty more.

And since to look at things in bloom
Fifty springs are little room,
About the woodlands I will go
To see the cherry hung with snow.

A. E. Housman

LEFT: *Cherry trees in Charlton, Worcestershire*

BELOW: *Cherry blossom, Great Kingshill, Buckinghamshire, April 24, 1937*

PIKE

Pike, three inches long, perfect
Pike in all parts, green tigering the gold.
Killers from the egg: the malevolent aged grin.
They dance on the surface among the flies.

Or move, stunned by their own grandeur,
Over a bed of emerald, silhouette
Of submarine delicacy and horror.
A hundred feet long in their world.

In ponds, under the heat-struck lily pads –
Gloom of their stillness:
Logged on last year's black leaves, watching upward
Or hung in an amber cavern of weeds

The jaws' hooked clamp and fangs
Not to be changed at this date;
A life subdued to its instrument;
The gills kneading quietly, and the pectorals.

Three we kept behind glass,
Jungled in weed: three inches, four,
And four and a half: fed fry to them –
Suddenly there were two. Finally one.

With a sag belly and the grin it was born with.
And indeed they spare nobody.
Two, six pounds each, over two feet long
High and dry and dead in the willow-herb –

One jammed past its gills down the other's gullet:
The outside eye stared: as a vice locks –
The same iron in this eye
Though its film shrank in death.

A pond I fished, fifty yards across,
Whose lilies and muscular tench
Had outlasted every visible stone
Of the monastery that planted them –

Stilled legendary depth:
It was as deep as England. It held
Pike too immense to stir, so immense and old
That past nightfall I dared not cast

But silently cast and fished
With the hair frozen on my head
For what might move, for what eye might move.
The still splashes on the dark pond,

Owls hushing the floating woods
Frail on my ear against the dream
Darkness beneath night's darkness had freed,
That rose slowly towards me, watching.

Ted Hughes

RIGHT: *The River Chess at Chenies, Hertfordshire, 1933*

OTTER

High in the dusk
I stand on a bridge,
bats like shuttles
flinging invisible
nets beneath arches

Something pops
the river's membrane:
black snout, flat head,
fluted fur streaming,
a disappearance.

The surface heals
and slides downstream,
my eyes alert
for the place, the next
door out of the deep.

As long as I search
it will not open;
my ears straining
at thin air for a plop,
a chirp, a whistle.

Nothing breaks
surface or silence;
still, I am drawn into
its element, this last-light
luminescence,

the web and flux
of worlds contained
in jet eyes, waiting
for a skinful of gold,
a naked whisker.

Paul Hyland

RIGHT: *The River Stour at Wimborne, Dorset*

FOLLOWER

My father worked with a horse-plough,
His shoulders globed like a full sail strung
Between the shafts and the furrow.
The horse strained at his clicking tongue.

An expert. He would set the wing
And fit the bright steel-pointed sock.
The sod rolled over without breaking.
At the headrig, with a single pluck

Of reins, the sweating team turned round
And back into the land. His eye
Narrowed and angled at the ground,
Mapping the furrow exactly.

I stumbled in his hob-nailed wake,
Fell sometimes on the polished sod;
Sometimes he rode me on his back
Dipping and rising to his plod.

I wanted to grow up and plough,
To close one eye, stiffen my arm.
All I ever did was follow
In his broad shadow round the farm.

I was a nuisance, tripping, falling,
Yapping always. But today
It is my father who keeps stumbling
Behind me, and will not go away.

Seamus Heaney

LEFT: *Cutting corn on the slopes of Shaldon Hill, Devon, 1937*

ABOVE: *Ploughing in Farningham, Kent, March 25, 1937*

TIDES

There are some coasts
Where the sea comes in spectacularly
Throwing itself up gullies, challenging cliffs,
Filling the harbours with great swirls and flourish,
A theatrical event that people gather for
Curtain up twice daily. You need to know
The hour of its starting, you have to be on guard.
There are other places
Places where you do not really notice
The gradual stretch of the fertile silk of water
No gurgling or dashings here, no froth no pounding
Only at some point the echo may sound different
And looking by chance one sees 'Oh the tide is in.'

Jenny Joseph

BELOW: *Beachcombers, Great Yarmouth, 1933*   RIGHT: *Eddystone Lighthouse, near Plymouth, January 15, 1934*

TO AUTUMN

Season of mists and mellow fruitfulness,
    Close bosom-friend of the maturing sun;
Conspiring with him how to load and bless
    With fruit the vines that round the thatch-eves run;
To bend with apples the moss'd cottage-trees,
    And fill all fruit with ripeness to the core;
        To swell the gourd, and plump the hazel shells
    With a sweet kernel; to set budding more,
And still more, later flowers for the bees,
Until they think warm days will never cease,
        For summer has o'er-brimm'd their clammy cells.

Who hath not seen thee oft amid thy store?
    Sometimes whoever seeks abroad may find
Thee sitting careless on a granary floor,
    Thy hair soft-lifted by the winnowing wind;
Or on a half-reap'd furrow sound asleep,
    Drows'd with the fume of poppies, while thy hook
        Spares the next swath and all its twined flowers:
And sometimes like a gleaner thou dost keep
    Steady thy laden head across a brook;
    Or by a cyder-press, with patient look,
        Thou watchest the last oozings hours by hours.

Where are the songs of spring? Ay, where are they?
    Think not of them, thou hast thy music too –
While barred clouds bloom the soft-dying day,
    And touch the stubble-plains with rosy hue;
Then in a wailful choir the small gnats mourn
    Among the river sallows, borne aloft
        Or sinking as the light wind lives or dies;
And full-grown lambs loud bleat from hilly bourn;
    Hedge-crickets sing; and now with treble soft
    The red-breast whistles from a garden-croft,
        And gathering swallows twitter in the skies.

John Keats

LEFT: *Gathering fruit, Seabrooks Farm, Chelmsford*

RIGHT: *Autumn in Burnham Beeches, Buckinghamshire, November 14, 1938*

IS MY TEAM PLOUGHING
POEM XXVII FROM A SHROPSHIRE LAD

'Is my team ploughing,
    That I was used to drive
And hear the harness jingle
    When I was man alive?'

Ay, the horses trample,
    The harness jingles now;
No change though you lie under
    The land you used to plough.

'Is football playing
    Along the river shore,
With lads to chase the leather,
    Now I stand up no more?'

Ay, the ball is flying,
    The lads play heart and soul;
The goal stands up, the keeper
    Stands up to keep the goal.

'Is my girl happy,
    That I thought hard to leave,
And has she tired of weeping
    As she lies down at eve?'

Ay, she lies down lightly,
    She lies not down to weep:
Your girl is well contented.
    Be still, my lad, and sleep.

'Is my friend hearty,
    Now I am thin and pine,
And has he found to sleep in
    A better bed than mine?'

Yes, lad, I lie easy,
    I lie as lads would choose;
I cheer a dead man's sweetheart,
    Never ask me whose.

A. E. Housman

LEFT: *Harvesting in Hamsey, Sussex, August 20, 1936*   ABOVE: *Ploughing on the Sussex Downs, October 15, 1936*

SEA-FEVER

I must go down to the seas again,
to the lonely sea and the sky,
And all I ask is a tall ship
and a star to steer her by,
And the wheel's kick and the wind's song
and the white sail's shaking,
And a grey mist on the sea's face
and a grey dawn breaking.

I must go down to the seas again,
for the call of the running tide
Is a wild call and a clear call
that may not be denied;
And all I ask is a windy day
with the white clouds flying,
And the flung spray and the blown spume,
and the sea-gulls crying.

I must go down to the seas again
to the vagrant gypsy life,
To the gull's way and the whale's way
where the wind's like a whetted knife;
And all I ask is a merry yarn
from a laughing fellow rover,
And quiet sleep and a sweet dream
when the long trick's over.

John Masefield

RIGHT: *Sunset at Land's End, October 20, 1933*

THE WAY THROUGH THE WOODS

They shut the road through the woods
Seventy years ago.
Weather and rain have undone it again,
And now you would never know
There was once a road through the woods
Before they planted the trees.

It is underneath the coppice and heath
And the thin anemones.
Only the keeper sees
That, where the ring-dove broods,
And the badgers roll at ease,
There was once a road through the woods.

Yet, if you enter the woods
Of a summer evening late,
When the night-air cools on the trout-ringed pools
Where the otter whistles his mate,
(They fear not men in the woods,
Because they see so few)
You will hear the beat of a horse's feet,
And the swish of a skirt in the dew,
Steadily cantering through
The misty solitudes,
As though they perfectly knew
The old lost road through the woods…
But there is no road through the woods.

Rudyard Kipling

LEFT: *Wimbledon Common,*
September 27, 1928

SPARROW

He's no artist
His taste in clothes is more
dowdy than gaudy.
And his nest – that blackbird, writing
pretty scrolls on the air with the gold nib of his beak
would call it a slum.

To stalk solitary on lawns,
to sing solitary in midnight trees,
to glide solitary over grey Atlantics –
not for him: he'd rather
a punch up in a gutter.

He carries what learning he has
lightly – it is, in fact, based only
on the usefulness whose result
is survival. A proletarian bird.
No scholar.

But when winter soft-shoes in
and these other birds –
ballet dancers, musicians, architects –
die in the snow
and freeze to branches,
watch him happily flying
on the O-levels and A-levels
of the air.

Norman MacCaig

RIGHT: *Spring in St. James's Park, London, March 15, 1961*

THE PASSIONATE SHEPHERD TO HIS LOVE

Come live with me and be my love,
And we will all the pleasures prove
That valleys, groves, hills, and fields,
Woods, or steepy mountain yields.

And we will sit upon rocks,
Seeing the shepherds feed their flocks
By shallow rivers to whose falls
Melodious birds sing madrigals.

And I will make thee beds of roses
And a thousand fragrant posies,
A cap of flowers, and a kirtle,
Embroidered all with leaves of myrtle.

A gown made of the finest wool
Which from our pretty lambs we pull,
Fair lined slippers for the cold,
With buckles of the purest gold.

A belt of straw and ivy buds,
With coral clasps and amber studs,
And if these pleasures may thee move,
Come live with me, and be my love.

The Shepherd's swains shall dance and sing
For thy delight each May morning.
If these delights thy mind may move,
Then live with me and be my love.

Christopher Marlowe

LEFT: *Shaldon Hill, Devon, 1936*

RIGHT: *To pastures new, February 10, 1936, Hertfordshire*

ON THE DOWNS

Up on the downs the red-eyed kestrels hover,
Eyeing the grass.
The field-mouse flits like a shadow into cover
As their shadows pass.

Men are burning the gorse on the down's shoulder;
A drift of smoke
Glitters with fire and hangs, and the skies smoulder,
And the lungs choke.

Once the tribe did thus on the downs, on these downs burning
Men in the frame.
Crying to the gods of the downs till their brains were turning
And the gods came.

And to-day on the downs, in the wind, the hawks, the grasses,
In the blood and air,
Something passes me and cries as it passes.
On the chalk downland bare.

John Masefield

BELOW: *The Gibbet Post on Inkpen Beacon, Berkshire*   RIGHT: *Sunrise over the Welsh mountains, August 24, 1935*

SHILOH – A REQUIEM

Skimming lightly, wheeling still,
  The swallows fly low
Over the field in clouded days,
  The forest-field of Shiloh –
Over the field where April rain
Solaced the parched one stretched in pain
Through the pause of night
That followed the Sunday fight
  Around the church of Shiloh –
The church so lone, the log-built one,
That echoed to many a parting groan
  And natural prayer
  Of dying foemen mingled there –
Foemen at morn, but friends at eve –
  Fame or country least their care:
(What like a bullet can undeceive!)
  But now they lie low,
While over them the swallows skim,
  And all is hushed at Shiloh.

Herman Melville

THIS PAGE: *Village of Mugerhanger, Bedfordshire*

RIGHT: *Chipping Campden, Gloucestershire, April 26, 1935*

THE HAWK

'Call down the hawk from the air;
Let him be hooded or caged
Till the yellow eye has grown mild,
For larder and spit are bare,
The old cook enraged,
The scullion gone wild.'

'I will not be clapped in a hood,
Nor a cage, nor alight upon wrist,
Now I have learnt to be proud
Hovering over the wood
In the broken mist
Or tumbling cloud.'

'What tumbling cloud did you cleave,
Yellow-eyed hawk of the mind,
Last evening? that I, who had sat
Dumbfounded before a knave,
Should give to my friend
A pretence of wit.'

William Butler Yeats

LEFT: *Loch Leven, Glencoe*

CORNISH CLIFFS

Those moments, tasted once and never done,
Of long surf breaking in the mid-day sun.
A far-off blow-hole booming like a gun–

The seagulls plane and circle out of sight
Below this thirsty, thrift-encrusted height,
The veined sea-campion buds burst into white

And gorse turns tawny orange, seen beside
Pale drifts of primroses cascading wide
To where the slate falls sheer into the tide.

More than in gardened Surrey, nature spills
A wealth of heather, kidney-vetch and squills
Over these long-defended Cornish hills.

A gun-emplacement of the latest war
Looks older than the hill fort built before
Saxon or Norman headed for the shore.

And in the shadowless, unclouded glare
Deep blue above us fades to whiteness where
A misty sea-line meets the wash of air.

Nut-smell of gorse and honey-smell of ling
Waft out to sea the freshness of the spring
On sunny shallows, green and whispering.

The wideness which the lark-song gives the sky
Shrinks at the clang of sea-birds sailing by
Whose notes are tuned to days when seas are high.

From today's calm, the lane's enclosing green
Leads inland to a usual Cornish scene
Slate cottages with sycamore between.
Small fields and tellymasts and wires and poles
With, as the everlasting ocean rolls,
Two chapels built for half a hundred souls.

John Betjeman

LEFT: *St. Michael's Mount, near Penzance, Cornwall, July 24, 1933*

RIGHT: *Bude, Cornwall, September 10, 1931*

SHOREHAM WALK

We walked
up through the wood
nettles and oak
a dark green
fall of light
leading us
past soft
erect wheat
then the white
potato flowers
and flints, a few
rusty can tops
it is the shining
June day, warm
as seldom

in our country
on our skin
a south wind
silver barley ears
are swaying
swaying us
and a lark
less visible than
the flower, blue
big, no bigger
than your pupil
under crusty
oaks again, ferns
they smell of salt
curved seawaves & a place

we found
called the kingdom
of children
you said, because
nobody frowns
as you climbed
vanishing up
a giant beech, red
as old blood
tall as the sky,
so many strong
branches it
was easy

Christopher Middleton

ABOVE: *Looking towards the Thames Valley over ripening wheat in Blewsbury*   RIGHT: *Savernake Forest, Wiltshire, 1936*

NEW ENGLISH LANDSCAPES

Their names are English names, the hills
Inscrutable through sheets of rain
Stay sulking under clouds until
The spotlight sun comes out again
To trace the trickles on their spines
Of rushing becks from ironstone mines
That wend and widen down the lea
To feed the farms that skirt the sea.

Their names are English ones – and old:
Tinwistle, Longstone, 'down' or 'wold'
Some Saxon lad or Norseman came
To hang each landmark with its name
When gazing from an autumn hill
While gales stripped a rusting wood
He never thought: "A science park
- or football stadium might be good."

Too soon the rambling lorries come
The worker ants with safety hats
The cranes the diggers and the pipes
The planners and the technocrats
Put up some dreadful edifice
A deal done behind closed doors
By coffee-quaffing metro-yobs
Who specialise in bending laws.

The wind won't dawdle on the moors
The Wordworths and the Brontes knew
But slices down the carriageway
To chill the ministers today
And those locations on their maps
Their names are English names, I'm told.
Which won't mean much to busy chaps
Tinwistle, Longstone, 'down' or 'wold'.

Martin Newell

LEFT: *Bolton Abbey, Wharfedale, Yorkshire, March 19, 1940*   BELOW: *The Long Man at Wilmington, Sussex*

SEASCAPE

Look, stranger, at this island now
The leaping light for your delight discovers,
Stand stable here
And silent be,
That through the channels of the ear
May wander like a river
The swaying sound of the sea.

Here at the small field's ending pause
Where the chalk wall falls to the foam, and its tall ledges
Oppose the pluck
And knock of the tide,
And the shingle scrambles after the sucking surf,
and the gull lodges
A moment on its sheer side.

Far off like floating seeds the ships
Diverge on urgent voluntary errands;
And the full view
Indeed may enter
And move in memory as now these clouds do,
That pass the harbour mirror
And all the summer through the water saunter.

W. H. Auden

LEFT: *Rough seas on the Yorkshire coast, December 15, 1933*

ABOVE: *La Corbiere Lighthouse, Jersey, October 11, 1938*

WALL

The wall walks the fell –
Grey millipede on slow
Stone hooves:
Its slack back hollowed
At gulleys and grooves
Or shouldering over
Old boulders
Too big to be rolled away.
Fallen fragments
Of the high crags
Crawl in the walk of the wall.

A dry-stone wall
Is a wall and a wall
Leaning together
(Cumberland-and-
Westmorland
Champion wrestlers),
Greening and weathering,

Flank by flank,
With filling of rubble
Between the two –
A double-rank
Stone dyke:
Flags and through –
stones jutting out sideways,
Like the steps of a stile.

A wall walks slowly,
At each give of the ground,
Each creak of the rock's ribs,
It puts its foot gingerly,
Arches its hog-holes,
Lets cobble and knee-joint
Settle and grip.
As the slippery fellside
Erodes and drifts,
The wall shifts with it,
Is always on the move.

They built a wall slowly,
A day a week;
Built it to stand,
But not stand still.
They built a wall to walk.

Norman Nicholson

ABOVE: *Looking towards Bunster Hill, Staffordshire, 1936*

RIGHT: *Cotswold walls and a beech wood near Aldsworth, Gloucestershire*

BLACKBERRYING

Nobody in the lane, and nothing, nothing but blackberries,
Blackberries on either side, though on the right mainly,
A blackberry alley, going down in hooks, and a sea
Somewhere at the end of it, heaving. Blackberries
Big as the ball of my thumb, and dumb as eyes
Ebon in the hedges, fat
With blue-red juices. These they squander on my fingers.
I had not asked for such a blood sisterhood; they must love me.
They accommodate themselves to my milkbottle, flattening their sides.

Overhead go the choughs in black, cacophonous flocks –
Bits of burnt paper wheeling in a blown sky.
Theirs is the only voice, protesting, protesting.
I do not think the sea will appear at all.
The high, green meadows are glowing, as if lit from within.
I come to one bush of berries so ripe it is a bush of flies,
Hanging their bluegreen bellies and their wing panes in a Chinese screen.
The honey-feast of the berries has stunned them; they believe in heaven.
One more hook, and the berries and bushes end.

The only thing to come now is the sea.
From between two hills a sudden wind funnels at me,
Slapping its phantom laundry in my face.
These hills are too green and sweet to have tasted salt.
I follow the sheep path between them. A last hook brings me
To the hills' northern face, and the face is orange rock
That looks out on nothing, nothing but a great space
Of white and pewter lights, and a din like silversmiths
Beating and beating at an intractable metal.

Sylvia Plath

ABOVE: *Blackberry picking, Croydon, Surrey, September 11, 1929*

RIGHT: *Roding Doe, Essex*

SHEPHERDS

Night of the black moon.
Above the house, Venus
bright as a lamp.
The field glitters in the flashlight
with the thirty stars of their eyes.

Somewhere the croak of a bird
and far off, chained
in the yard of a nameless farm
a dog barks. Downwind
the smoke of our dying fire.

In the unsteady light of the torch
you shoulder the bale, break it,
ram the racks with the needling sweetness
of nettle-scents, herbs, the trapped breath
of thirteen kinds of summer grasses.

The ewes are pushy,
Blackface first to the bucket,
then the one who hooves our shoulders
to hurry the mumble
of our iron hands.

You call from the dark –
first lambs steaming in lamplight.
We carry them in, one each, hot and yolky
with their strange scent of the sea,
the ewe in a panic at our heels.

Above us in the Square of Pegasus
a satellite wavers
like torch in a field.

Gillian Clarke

LEFT: *Sheep grazing in the village of Ripe, Sussex, January 21, 1932*   BELOW: *Ohio, November 23, 1931*

125

THE SINGING CAT

It was a little captive cat
Upon a crowded train
His mistress takes him from his box
To ease his fretful pain

She holds him tight upon her knee
The graceful animal
All the people look at him
He is so beautiful

But oh he pricks and oh he prods
And turns upon her knee
Then lifteth up his innocent voice
In plaintive melody

He lifteth up his innocent voice
He lifteth up, he singeth
And to each human countenance
A smile of grace he bringeth

He lifteth up his innocent paw
Upon her breast he clingeth
And everybody cries, Behold
The cat, the cat that singeth.

He lifteth up his innocent voice
He lifteth up, he singeth
And all the people warm themselves
In the love his beauty bringeth.

Stevie Smith

THIS PAGE: *Dunstable Down, Bedfordshire, 1936*

THE FROG PRINCE

I am a frog
I live under a spell
I live at the bottom
of a green well.

And here I must wait
Until a maiden places me
On her royal pillow
And kisses me
In her father's palace.

The story is familiar
Everybody knows it well
But do other enchanted people feel as nervous
As I do? The stories do not tell,

Ask if they will be happier
When the changes come
As already they are fairly happy
in a frogs doom?

I have been a frog now
For a hundred years
And in all this time
I have not shed many tears,

I am happy, I like the life,
Can swim for many a mile
(When I have hopped to the river)
And am for ever agile.
And the quietness,

Yes, I like to be quiet
I am habituated
To a quiet life,

But always when I think these thoughts
As I sit in my well
Another thought comes to me and says:
It is part of the spell

To be happy
To work up contentment
To make much of being a frog
To fear disenchantment.

Says, it will be heavenly
To be set free,
Cries, Heavenly the girl who disenchants
And the royal times, heavenly
And I think it will be.

Come then, royal girl and royal times,
Come quickly,
I can be happy until you come
But I cannot be heavenly,
Only disenchanted people
Can be heavenly.

Stevie Smith

THE EAGLE

He clasps the crag with crooked hands;
Close to the sun in lonely lands,
Ringed with the azure world, he stands.

The wrinkled sea beneath him crawls;
He watches from his mountain walls,
And like a thunderbolt he falls.

Alfred, Lord Tennyson

RIGHT: *A view of the Spittal Hotel, Glenshee, Perthshire, October 22, 1935*

THE PUZZLED GAME BIRDS

They are not those who used to feed us
When we were young – they cannot be
These shapes that now bereave and bleed us?
They are not those who used to feed us,
For did we then cry, they would heed us.
– If hearts can house such treachery
They are not those who used to feed us
When we were young – they cannot be!

Thomas Hardy

LEFT: *Grouse shoot at Riemore, East Perthshire, August 14, 1934*

ABOVE: *Grouse shoot on Reeth High Moor, Yorkshire, August 23, 1933*

131

REQUIEM

Under the wide and starry sky
Dig the grave and let me lie.
Glad did I live and gladly die,
    And I laid me down with a will.

This be the verse you grave for me:
Here he lies where he longed to be;
Home is the sailor, home from the sea,
    And the hunter home from the hill.

Robert Louis Stevenson

ABOVE: *Sunset over the sea, December 31, 1935*   RIGHT: *Ben Venue and Loch Katrine, Perthshire*

THE BANKS O' DOON

Ye flowery banks o'bonnie Doon,
 How can ye blume sae fair;
How can ye chant, ye little birds,
 And I sae fu'o'care!
Thou'll break my heart, thou bonnie bird
 That sings upon the bough;
Thou minds me o'the happy days
 When my fause luve was true.
Thou'll break my heart, thou bonnie bird
 That sings beside thy mate;
For sae I sat, and sae I sang,
 And wist na o'my fate.
Aft hae I rov'd by bonnie Doon,

To see the wood-bine twine,
And ilka bird sang o'its love,
 And sae did I o'mine.
Wi'lightsome heart I pu'd a rose
 Frae aff its thorny tree,
And my fause luver staw the rose,
 But left the thorn wi'me.
Wi'lightsome heart I pu'd a rose,
 Upon a mom in June:
And sae I flourish'd on the morn,
 And sae was pu'd or noon!

Robert Burns

RIGHT: *Sunset at Loch Long, Dumbartonshire, December 30, 1936* ABOVE: *Rydal Water, Cumbria*

SKETCH

The shadows of the ships
Rock on the crest
In the low blue lustre
Of the tardy and the soft inrolling tide.
A long brown bar at the dip of the sky
Puts an arm of sand in the span of salt.
The lucid and endless wrinkles
Draw in, lapse and withdraw.
Wavelets crumble and white spent bubbles
Wash on the floor of the beach.
   Rocking on the crest
   In the low blue lustre
   Are the shadows of the ships.

Carl Sandburg

ABOVE: *Sunset over the Moray Firth, Banffshire, April 14, 1937*

RIGHT: *Waves breaking against Beachy Head, January 25, 1935*

PEBBLES

Talking was difficult. Instead
we gathered coloured pebbles
from the places on the beach
where they occurred.

They were sea-smoothed, sea-completed.
They enclosed what they intended
to mean in shapes
as random and necessary
as the shapes of words

and when finally
we spoke
the sounds of our voices fell
into the air   single and
solid and rounded and really
there
and then dulled, and then like sounds
gone,   a fistful of gathered
pebbles there was no point
in taking home, dropped on a beachful
of other coloured pebbles

and when we turned to go
a flock of small
birds flew scattered by the
fright of our sudden moving
and disappeared: hard

sea pebbles
thrown solid for an instant
against the sky

flight of words

Margaret Atwood

ABOVE: *Waves on the Mevagissey Coast, Cornwall, August 9, 1938*

LEFT: *First sight of the sea, 1946*

SHALL I COMPARE THEE
TO A SUMMER'S DAY?

Shall I compare thee to a summer's day?
Thou art more lovely and more temperate:
Rough winds do shake the darling buds of May,
And summer's lease hath all too short a date:
Sometime too hot the eye of heaven shines,
And often is his gold complexion dimm'd:
And every fair from fair sometime declines,
By chance or nature's changing course untrimm'd;
But thy eternal summer shall not fade
Nor lose possession of that fair thou ow'st,
Nor shall death brag thou wander'st in his shade,
When in eternal lines to time thou grow'st:
So long as men can breathe, or eyes can see,
So long lives this, and this gives life to thee.

William Shakespeare

LEFT: *River Ply at Plymbridge, Devon, May 25, 1936*

ABOVE: *Grove Mill, Cassiobury Park, Watford, Hertfordshire, May 16, 1933*

WINTER-PIECE

You wake, all windows blind – embattled sprays
grained on the medieval glass.
Gates snap like gunshot
as you handle them. Five-barred fragility
sets flying fifteen rooks who go together
silently ravenous about this winter-piece
that will not feed them. They alight
beyond, scavenging, missing everything
but the bladed atmosphere, the white resistance.
Ruts with iron flanges track
through a hard decay
Where you discern once more
oak-leaf by hawthorn, for the frost
rewhets their edges. In a perfect web
blanched along each spoke
and circle of its woven wheel,
the spider hangs, grasp unbroken
And death-masked in cold. Returning
you see the house glint-out behind
its holed and ragged glaze,
frost-fronds all streaming.

Charles Tomlinson

RIGHT: *Snow scene in the Derbyshire hills*

TO A SKYLARK

(Extract)

Hail to thee, blithe Spirit!
Bird thou never wert,
That from Heaven, or near it,
Pourest thy full heart
In profuse strains of unpremeditated art.

Higher still and higher
From the earth thou springest
Like a cloud of fire;
The blue deep thou wingest,
And singing still dost soar, and soaring ever singest.

In the golden lightning
Of the sunken sun,
O'er which clouds are bright'ning,
Thou dost float and run;
Like an unbodied joy whose race is just begun.

The pale purple even
Melts around thy flight;
Like a star of Heaven,
In the broad daylight
Thou art unseen, but yet I hear thy shrill delight.
Keen as are the arrows
Of that silver sphere,

Whose intense lamp narrows
In the white dawn clear
Until we hardly see – we feel that it is there.

All the earth and air
With thy voice is loud,
As, when night is bare,
From one lonely cloud
The moon rains out her beams, and Heaven is
                                        overflowed.

What thou art we know not;
What is most like thee?
From rainbow clouds there flow not
Drops so bright to see
As from thy presence showers a rain of melody.

Percy Bysshe Shelley

THE WINDHOVER

To Christ our Lord

I caught this morning morning's minion, king –
   dom of daylight's dauphin, dapple-dawn-drawn Falcon, in his riding
   Of the rolling level underneath him steady air, and striding
High there, how he rung upon the rein of a wimpling wing
In his ecstasy! then off, off forth on swing,
   As a skate's heel sweeps smooth on a bow-bend: the hurl and gliding
   Rebuffed the big wind. My heart in hiding
Stirred for a bird, – the achieve of, the mastery of the thing!

Brute beauty and valour and act, oh, air, pride, plume, here
   Buckle! AND the fire that breaks from thee then, a billion
Times told lovelier, more dangerous, O my chevalier!

   No wonder of it: shéer plód makes plough down sillion
Shine, and blue-bleak embers, ah my dear,
   Fall, gall themselves, and gash gold-vermilion.

Gerard Manley Hopkins

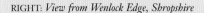

RIGHT: *View from Wenlock Edge, Shropshire*

THE HOLLOW WOOD

Out in the sun the goldfinch flits
Along the thistle-tops, flits and twits
Above the hollow wood
Where birds swim like fish
Fish that laugh and shriek
To and fro, far below
In the pale hollow wood.

Lichen, ivy, and moss
Keep evergreen the trees
That stand half-flayed and dying,
And the dead trees on their knees
In dog's-mercury, and moss:
And the bright twit of the goldfinch drops
Down there as he flits on thistle-tops.

Edward Thomas

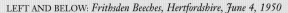

LEFT AND BELOW: *Frithsden Beeches, Hertfordshire, June 4, 1950*

I SAW IN LOUISIANA
A LIVE OAK GROWING

I saw in Louisiana a live-oak growing,

All alone stood it, and the moss hung down from the branches;

Without any companion it grew there uttering joyous leaves of dark green,

And its look, rude, unbending, lusty, made me think of myself,

But I wonder'd how it could utter joyous leaves, standing alone there,
    without its friend near, for I knew I could not,

And I broke off a twig with a certain number of leaves upon it, and
    twined around it a little moss,

And brought it away, and I have placed it in sight in my room,

It is not needed to remind me as of my own dear friends,

(For I believe lately I think of little else than of them;)

Yet it remains to me a curious token – it makes me think of manly love,

For all that, and though the live-oak glistens there in Louisiana,
    solitary, in a wide flat space,

Uttering joyous leaves all its life without a friend a lover near,

I know very well I could not.

Walt Whitman

LEFT: *Oak tree in Richmond Park,*
August 2, 1935

RIGHT: *Sherwood Forest*

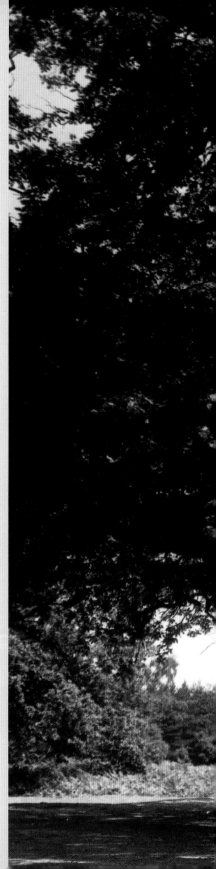

150

FARM CHILD

Look at this village boy, his head is stuffed
With all the nests he knows, his pockets with flowers,
Snail-shells and bits of glass, the fruit of hours
Spent in the fields by thorn and thistle tuft.
Look at his eyes see the harebell hiding there;
Mark how the sun has freckled his smooth face
Like a finch's egg under that bush of hair
That dares the wind, and in the mixen now
Notice his poise; from such unconscious grace
Earth breeds and beckons to the stubborn plough.

R. S. Thomas

ABOVE: *Butterflies in Long Buckby, Northamptonshire, September 8, 1947*

HEDGEHOG

Twitching the leaves just where the drainpipe clogs
In ivy leaves and mud, purposeful
Creature at night about its business. Dogs
Fear his stiff seriousness. He chews away

At beetles, worms, slugs, frogs. Can kill a hen
With one snap of his jaws, can taunt a snake
To death on muscled spines. Old countrymen
Tell tales of hedgehogs sucking a cow dry.

But this one, cramped by houses, fences, walls
Must have slept here all winter in that heap
Of compost, or have inched by intervals
Through tidy gardens to this ivy bed.

And here, dim-eyed, but ears so sensitive
A voice within the house can make him freeze,
He scuffs he edge of danger; yet can live
Happily in our nights and absences.

A country creature, wary, quiet and shrewd,
He takes the milk we give him, when we're gone.
At night, our slamming voices must seem crude
To one who sits and waits for silences.

Anthony Thwaite

RIGHT: *Frithsden Beeches near Ashridge, Hertfordshire*

154

ON WENLOCK EDGE THE WOOD'S IN TROUBLE

POEM XXXI FROM A SHROPSHIRE LAD

On Wenlock Edge the wood's in trouble;
    His forest fleece the Wrekin heaves;
The gale, it plies the saplings double,
    And thick on Severn snow the leaves.

'Twould blow like this through holt and hanger
    When Uricon the city stood:
'Tis the old wind in the old anger,
    But then it threshed another wood.

Then, 'twas before my time, the Roman
    At yonder heaving hill would stare:
The blood that warms an English yeoman,
    The thoughts that hurt him, they were there.

There, like the wind through woods in riot,
    Through him the gale of life blew high;
The tree of man was never quiet:
    Then 'twas the Roman, now 'tis I.

The gale, it plies the saplings double,
    It blows so hard, 'twill soon be gone:
To-day the Roman and his trouble
    Are ashes under Uricon.

A. E. Housman

ABOVE: *Much Wenlock Abbey, Shropshire*

RIGHT: *Wenlock Edge and the Wrekin, Shropshire*

THE DALLIANCE OF THE EAGLES

Skirting the river road, (my forenoon walk, my rest,)
Skyward in air a sudden muffled sound, the dalliance of the eagles,
The rushing amorous contact high in space together,
The clinching interlocking claws, a living, fierce, gyrating wheel,
Four beating wings, two beaks, a swirling mass tight grappling,
In tumbling turning clustering loops, straight downward falling,
Till o'er the river pois'd, the twain yet one, a moment's lull,
A motionless still balance in the air, then parting, talons loosing,
Upward again on slow-firm pinions slanting, their separate diverse flight,
She hers, he his, pursuing.

Walt Whitman

LEFT: *Mountain in Glencoe*

159

RAIN

Rain, midnight rain, nothing but the wild rain
On this bleak hut, and solitude, and me
Remembering again that I shall die
And neither hear the rain nor give it thanks
For washing me cleaner than I have been
Since I was born into this solitude.
Blessed are the dead that the rain rains upon:
But here I pray that none whom once I loved
Is dying tonight or lying still awake
Solitary, listening to the rain,

Either in pain or thus in sympathy
Helpless among the living and the dead,
Like a cold water among broken reeds,
Myriads of broken reeds all still and stiff,
Like me who have no love which this wild rain
Has not dissolved except the love of death,
If love it be for what is perfect and
Cannot, the tempest tells me, disappoint.

Edward Thomas

ABOVE: *London Zoo, August 5, 1952*   RIGHT: *River Misbourne, Chalfont St. Giles, Buckinghamshire, February 25, 1937*

OWL

His face is concave
to focus sound,

a radio-telescope
in quills,
the countenance of radar.

Each feather
is silent as a moth,
his body
stuffed with wool and fur,
a lover of soft coats
lined in scarlet,

a flying wardrobe
with hooks.

His call hangs
full-moon on branches.

He's round,
a tea-cosy ribbed
in white, grey and brown.

Who could believe
his needles knit blood?

Isobel Thrilling

THE NORTH SEA IN THE AUTUMN

This is the sea the sailor saw
Which thrashed the shingle on the shore
Swallowed sloops and galleons whole
Yet gave up herrings by the shoal
The 'silver treasure' called by men
Built Blythburgh – a fish church then
Paid for its windows and chimeres
Though took back Dunwich in arrears

This is the sea of winter geese
Its gun-grey, bird-limed, heaving fleece
The Whale Road where the Saxons went
To settle Suffolk, Essex, Kent.
Cold currents fetched the codfish down
Filled ketches, smacks and fed the town
And sped the skillingers to bring
The oysters back from Terschelling

This was a sea of working ways
Of dirty, bleach-stained denim days
Where little ships from net-strewn quays
Their halliards rattling in the breeze
Set out with men in set-jawed mood
To turn their labours into food
Who knew, when fishing quotas bit
That nothing good could come of it

This was a sea of fish and birds
And all the figures, facts and words
On how its creatures disappear
Cannot convey its troubles here
– Nor any pious why-oh-whying.
The sea, the old North Sea is dying
And muffles in its warming swell
The tolling of the Dunwich bell.

Martin Newell

LEFT: *Waves breaking in the Channel, November 23, 1938*   BELOW: *Manorbier, Pembroke*

DAFFODILS

I wandered lonely as a cloud
That floats on high o'er vales and hills,
When all at once I saw a crowd,
A host of golden daffodils;
Beside the lake, beneath the trees,
Fluttering and dancing in the breeze.

Continuous as the stars that shine
And twinkle on the Milky Way,
They stretched in never-ending line
Along the margin of a bay:
Ten thousand saw I at a glance,
Tossing their heads in sprightly dance.

The waves beside them danced, but they
Out-did the sparkling waves in glee:
A Poet could not but be gay
In such a jocund company:
I gazed – and gazed – but little thought
What wealth the show to me had brought:

For oft, when on my couch I lie
In vacant or in pensive mood,
They flash upon that inward eye
Which is the bliss of solitude,
And then my heart with pleasure fills,
And dances with the daffodils.

William Wordsworth

RIGHT: *Picking daffodils near Redhill, Surrey, April 20, 1935*

LINES WRITTEN A FEW MILES ABOVE TINTERN ABBEY

(extract)

Five years have passed; five summers, with the length
Of five long winters! And again I hear
These waters, rolling from their mountain springs
With a soft inland murmur. Once again
Do I behold these steep and lofty cliffs,
That on a wild secluded scene impress
Thoughts of more deep seclusion; and connect
The landscape with the quiet of the sky.
The day is come when I again repose
Here, under this dark sycamore, and view
These plots of cottage-ground, these orchard-tufts,
Which at this season, with their unripe fruits,
Are clad in one green hue, and lose themselves
'Mid groves and copses. Once again I see
These hedgerows, hardly hedge-rows, little lines
Of sportive wood run wild: these pastoral farms,
Green to the very door; and wreaths of smoke
Sent up, in silence, from among the trees!
With some uncertain notice, as might seem
Of vagrant dwellers in the houseless woods,
Or of some hermit's cave, where by his fire
The hermit sits alone.

William Wordsworth

BELOW AND RIGHT: *Tintern Abbey, Monmouth, 1933*

THE THUNDERSTORM

When Coniston Old Man was younger
And his deep-quarried sides were stronger,
Goats may have leapt about Goat's Water;
But why the tarn that looks like its young daughter
Though lying high under the fell
Should be called Blind Tarn, who can tell?

For from Dow Crag, passing it by,
I saw it as a dark presageful eye;
And soon I knew that I was not mistaken
Hearing the thunder the loose echoes waken
About Scafell and Scafell Pike
And feeling the slant raindrops strike.

And when I came to Walna Pass
Hailstones hissing and hopping among the grass,
Beneath a rock I found a hole;
But with sharp crack and rumbling roll on roll
So quick the lightening came and went
The solid rock was like a lighted tent.

Andrew Young

175

ADLESTROP

Yes. I remember Adlestrop –
The name because one afternoon
Of heat the express-train drew up there
Unwontendly. It was late June.

The steam hissed. Some one cleared his throat.
No one left and no one came
On the bare platform. What I saw
Was Adlestrop – only the name

And willows, willow-herb, and grass,
And meadowsweet, and haycocks dry,
No whit less still and lonely fair
Than the high cloudlets in the sky.

And for that minute a blackbird sang
Close by, and round him, mistier,
Farther and farther, all the birds
Of Oxfordshire and Gloucestershire.

Edward Thomas

ABOVE: *Cranham, Gloucester*

RIGHT: *Blackbird in a nest in Bradford Park Conservatory, May 16, 1950*

THE WILD SWANS AT COOLE

The trees are in their autumn beauty,
The woodland paths are dry,
Under the October twilight the water
Mirrors a still sky;
Upon the brimming water among the stones
Are nine-and-fifty swans.

The nineteenth autumn has come upon me
Since I first made my count;
I saw, before I had well finished,
All suddenly mount
And scatter wheeling in great broken rings
Upon their clamorous wings.

I have looked upon those brilliant creatures,
And now my heart is sore.
All's changed since I, hearing at twilight,
The first time on this shore,
The bell-beat of their wings above my head,
Trod with a lighter tread.

Unwearied still, lover by lover,
They paddle in the cold
Companionable streams or climb the air;
Their hearts have not grown old;
Passion or conquest, wander where they will,
Attend upon them still.

But now they drift on the still water,
Mysterious, beautiful;
Among what rushes will they build,
By what lake's edge or pool
Delight men's eyes when I awake some day
To find they have flown away?

William Butler Yeats

RIGHT: *Highams Park Lake, Epping Forest, Essex,*
November 13, 1934

NIGHT MAIL

This is the Night Mail crossing the border,
Bringing the cheque and the postal order,
Letters for the rich, letters for the poor,
The shop at the corner and the girl next door.
Pulling up Beattock, a steady climb:
The gradient's against her, but she's on time.

Thro' sparse counties she rampages,
Her driver's eye upon the gauges.
Panting up past lonely farms
Fed by the fireman's restless arms.
Striding forward along the rails
Thro' southern uplands with northern mails.

Winding up the valley to the watershed,
Thro' the heather and the weather and the dawn overhead.
Past cotton-grass and moorland boulder
Shovelling white steam over her shoulder,
Snorting noisily as she passes
Silent miles of wind-bent grasses.

Birds turn their heads as she approaches,
Stare from the bushes at her blank-faced coaches.
Sheepdogs cannot turn her course;
They slumber on with paws across.
In the farm she passes no one wakes,
But a jug in the bedroom gently shakes.

Dawn freshens, the climb is done.
Down towards Glasgow she descends
Towards the steam tugs yelping down the glade of cranes,
Towards the fields of apparatus, the furnaces
Set on the dark plain like gigantic chessmen.
All Scotland waits for her:
In the dark glens, beside the pale-green sea lochs
Men long for news.
Letters of thanks, letters from banks,

Letters of joy from the girl and the boy,
Receipted bills and invitations
To inspect new stock or visit relations,
And applications for situations
And timid lovers' declarations
And gossip, gossip from all the nations,
News circumstantial, news financial,

Letters with holiday snaps to enlarge in,
Letters with faces scrawled in the margin,
Letters from uncles, cousins, and aunts,
Letters to Scotland from the South of France,
Letters of condolence to Highlands and Lowlands
Notes from overseas to Hebrides
Written on paper of every hue,
The pink, the violet, the white and the blue,
The chatty, the catty, the boring, adoring,
The cold and official and the heart's outpouring,
Clever, stupid, short and long,
The typed and the printed and the spelt all wrong.

Thousands are still asleep
Dreaming of terrifying monsters,
Or of friendly tea beside the band at
    Cranston's or Crawford's:
Asleep in working Glasgow, asleep in well-set Edinburgh,
Asleep in granite Aberdeen,
They continue their dreams,
And shall wake soon and long for letters,
And none will hear the postman's knock
Without a quickening of the heart,
For who can bear to feel himself forgotten?

W. H. Auden

LEFT: *Cliffs between Dover and Folkstone, January 13, 1937* BELOW: *Bridge over the River Tummel, Perthshire*

MARCH HARES

I made myself as a tree,
No withered leaf twirling on me;
No, not a bird that stirred my boughs,
As looking out from wizard brows
I watched those lithe and lovely forms
That raised the leaves in storms.

I watched them leap and run,
Their bodies hollowed in the sun
To thin transparency,
That I could clearly see
The shallow colour of their blood
Joyous in love's full flood.

I was content enough,
Watching that serious game of love,
That happy hunting in the wood
Where the pursuer was the more pursued,
To stand in breathless hush
With no more life myself than tree or bush.

Andrew Young

RIGHT: *Langdale Pikes,
The Lake District,
October 13, 1934*

TO A SQUIRREL AT
KYLE-NA-NO

Come play with me;
Why should you run
Through the shaking tree
As though I'd a gun
To strike you dead?
When all I would do
Is to scratch your head
And let you go.

William Butler Yeats

RIGHT: *Glory Woods, Surrey, July 25, 1925*

THE SWALLOWS

All day – when early morning shone
With every dewdrop its own dawn
And when cockchafers were abroad
Hurtling like missiles that had lost their road –

The swallows twisting here and there
Round unseen corners of the air
Upstream and down so quickly passed
I wondered that their shadows flew as fast.

They steeplechased over the bridge
And dropped down to a drowning midge
Sharing the river with the fish,
Although the air itself was their chief dish.

Blue-winged snowballs! until they turned
And then with ruddy breasts they burned;
All in one instant everywhere,
Jugglers with their own bodies in the air.

Andrew Young

I STOOD TIP-TOE UPON A LITTLE HILL

(extract)

I stood tip-toe upon a little hill,
The air was cooling, and so very still,
That the sweet buds which with a modest pride
Pull droopingly, in slanting curve aside,
Their scantly leaved, and finely tapering stems,
Had not yet lost those starry diadems
Caught from the early sobbing of the morn.
The clouds were pure and white as flocks new shorn,
And fresh from the clear brook; sweetly they slept
On the blue fields of heaven, and then there crept
A little noiseless noise among the leaves,
Born of the very sigh that silence heaves:
For not the faintest motion could be seen
Of all the shades that slanted o'er the green.
There was wide wand'ring for the greediest eye,
To peer about upon variety;
Far round the horizon's crystal air to skim,
And trace the dwindled edgings of its brim;

To picture out the quaint, and curious bending
Of a fresh woodland alley, never ending;
Or by the bowery clefts, and leafy shelves,
Guess where the jaunty streams refresh themselves.
I gazed awhile, and felt as light, and free
As though the fanning wings of Mercury
Had played upon my heels: I was light-hearted,
And many pleasures to my vision started;
So I straightway began to pluck a posey
Of luxuries bright, milky, soft and rosy.

A bush of May flowers with the bees about them;
Ah, sure no tasteful nook would be without them;
And let a lush laburnum oversweep them,
And let long grass grow round the roots to keep them
Moist, cool and green; and shade the violets,
That they may bind the moss in leafy nets.

John Keats

RIGHT: *River Wye above Rhayader, Radnorshire, 1933*

LEFT: *King's Park, Edinburgh, May 10, 1936.*

INDEX OF FIRST LINES

Acknowledgements

The editor and publishers acknowledge the copyright owners of the poems listed below with grateful thanks for permission to reproduce the works in this book.

John Agard: *In the Air* by John Agard. By permission of Bloodaxe Books.

Margaret Atwood: *Pebbles* from *Some Objects of Wood and Stone* from Eating Fire: Selected Poetry 1965-1995 by Margaret Atwood by permission of Little Brown Book Group.

W H Auden: *The Nightmail* and *Seascape*. Faber & Faber

John Betjeman: *Cornish Cliffs* and *Upper Lambourne* from Collected Poems, by John Betjeman © The Estate of John Betjeman 1955, 1958, 1962, 1964, 1968, 1970, 1979, 1981, 1982, 2001 Reproduced by permission of John Murray (Publishers).

Lawrence Binyon: *The Burning Of The Leaves*. The Society of Authors as the Literary Representative of the Estate of Laurence Binyon.

Charles Causley: *Green Man in the Garden* from Collected Poems for Children by Charles Causley published by Macmillan. By permission of David Higham Associates.

Gillian Clarke: *Shepherds* and *A Difficult Birth 1998*. Carcanet

Billy Collins: *In The Evening; Man In The Moon* and *The Wolf*. Pan Macmillan and Random House.

Wendy Cope: *Flowers*. Faber & Faber.

Idris Davies: *High Summer On The Mountains*. Faber & Faber.

Walter De La Mare: *Silver*. The Literary Trustees of Walter de la Mare and the Society of Authors as their representative.

Emily Dickinson: *Fame is a bee*. Little Brown Group, Hachette Book Group USA.

Robert Frost: *The Oven Bird, To Earthward* and *Stopping by Woods on a Snowy Evening* from the Poetry of Robert Frost edited by Edward Connery Latham. Published by Jonathan Cape. Reprinted by permission of the Random House Group Ltd.

Gillilan, Pamela: *Harvest*. By permission of Bloodaxe Books.

Seamus Heaney: *Badgers* and *Follower*. Faber & Faber.

Gerard Manley Hopkins: *Spring; The Starlight Night; The Windhover* and *Pied Beauty*. Oxford University Press.

Ted Hughes: *Pike* and *The Kingfisher*. Faber & Faber.

Paul Hyland: *Otter* from The Art of the Impossible, Bloodaxe Books 2004. By permission of David Higham Associates.

Jenny Joseph: *Tides*. Johnson & Alcock.

Rudyard Kipling: *The Way Through The Woods*. Macmillan and the National Trust.

Norman MacCaig: *Sparrow* and *Kingfisher*. Birlinn Limited.

John Masefield: *Sea Fever* and *Up On The Downs* The Society of Authors as the Literary Representative of John Masefield.

Christopher Middleton: *Shoreham Walk*, Carcanet.

Martin Newell: *New English Landscapes* and *The North Sea in Autumn*. Copyright Martin Newell, reproduced by permission of Martin Newell and Jardine Press Ltd

Norman Nicholson: *Wall*. Faber & Faber

Sylvia Plath: *Blackberrying*. Faber & Faber

Carl Sandburg: *Sketch* from Chicago Poems by Carl Sandburg, copyright 1916 by Holt, Rinehart and Winston and renewed 1944 by Carl Sandburg, reprinted by permission of Houghton Mifflin Harcourt Publishing Company.

Stevie Smith: *The Singing Cat* and *The Frog Prince* by Stevie Smith, from Collected Poems of Stevie Smith, copyright © 1966 by Stevie Smith. Reprinted by permission of New Directions Publishing Corp.

Dylan Thomas: *Fern Hill* from Collected Poems of Dylan Thomas published by Orion. By permission of David Higham Associates.

Edward Thomas: *Adlestrop, The Hollow Wood* and *Rain*. Adlestrop from Collected Poems of Edward Thomas Edited by R George Thomas, 1978. By permission of Oxford University Press Inc.

R S Thomas: *Farm Child*. Orion

Isobel Thrilling: *Owl*.

Anthony Thwaite: *Hedgehog*. Curtis Brown

Charles Tomlinson: *Winter-Piece*. Oxford University Press.

William Carlos Williams: *Queen Anne's Lace* by William Carlos Williams, from The Collected Poems: Volume 1, 1909 - 1939, by New Directions Publishing Corp. Reprinted by permission of New Directions Publishing Corp.

William Butler Yeats: *The Hawk, Lake Isle of Innisfree, The Song of Wandering Aengus, To A Squirrel At Kyle-Na-No* and *The Wild Swans at Coole*. Scribner Simon & Schuster.

Andrew Young: *March Hares, The Swallows* and *The Thunderstorm*. Carcanet.

Every reasonable effort has been made by the Publishers to trace copyright holders and in all cases where the copyright owner has been identified, permission to reproduce the work has been requested, but in some instances it may not have proved possible to locate or contact them. The publisher will be happy to rectify omissions or errors in future reprints and/or new editions.

The photographs in this book are from the archives of the *Daily Mail*. Thanks to all the staff, past and present.

Special thanks to Alan and Debby Pinnock, whose help, ideas and love of poetry made this book possible.

Thanks also to Gordon Mills, Cliff Salter, Melanie Cox, Alice Hill and Hannah Rickayzen.